His Hand
on Your
Shoulder

His Hand
on Your
Shoulder

Peter Marshall

Published by

chosen books

FLEMING H. REVELL COMPANY
OLD TAPPAN, NEW JERSEY

Library of Congress Cataloging-in-Publication Data

Marshall, Peter, 1902-1949.
  His hand on your shoulder / Peter Marshall.
     p.   cm.
  Collection of four sermons.
  ISBN 0-8007-9158-4
  1. Sermons, American. 2. Presbyterian Church—Sermons.
  I. Title.
  BX9178.M363H57 1990
  252'.05 — dc20 — dc20   89-
48718
                                            CIP

A Chosen Book
Copyright © 1990 by Leonard E. LeSourd

Chosen Books are published by
Fleming H. Revell Company
Old Tappan, New Jersey
Printed in the United States of America

Contents

1

UNDER SEALED ORDERS

I do not know what picture the phrase *under sealed orders* suggests to you.
To me it recalls very vividly a scene from the first World War, when I was a little boy spending vacations at a Scottish seaport.

I saw a gray destroyer slipping hurriedly from port in response to some urgent commands. . . .
I watched the crew hurry their preparations for sailing,

watched them cast off the mooring hawsers,
saw the sleek ship get under way, as she rose to meet the lazy ground swell of a summer evening.
Her Morse lamp was winking on the control bridge aft, and I watched her until she was lost in the mists of the North Sea.

She was a mystery vessel.
She had sailed under sealed orders.
Not even her officers knew her destination or the
point of rendezvous.
We all start out in life, going—we know not where.
It will be revealed later.
But meanwhile we must go out in faith—
     under sealed orders.

So, in like manner, all the pioneers of faith have
gone out—and all the explorers—
     Abraham of old
        Columbus
          Magellan
            John Smith
              Peary
                Lindbergh
                Byrd.

Abraham stands out among the Old Testament
heroes as the leading example of this kind of faith.
In the epistle to the Hebrews we are told:

> "By faith Abraham . . . went out, not knowing
> whither he went."   Hebrews 11:8

Here was Abraham, a mature and successful man, having established himself in Ur of the Chaldees. Then God spoke to him:

> "Get thee out of thy country, and from thy kindred, and from thy father's house, unto a land that I will shew thee: And I will make of thee a great nation, and I will bless thee, and make thy name great . . . and in thee shall all families of the earth be blessed."
>
> Genesis 12:1-3

Try to imagine what was involved in obeying this guidance. Abraham had to sever all his business connections

uproot himself

procure supplies for a new and strange way of life. He was giving up the comforts and conveniences of a world he knew to live as a nomad under canvas with no settled abode.

From a commonsense point of view, it was crazy. Doubtless Abraham had many friends who told him just that.

Where was he going?

Well, he did not know exactly.

What was he going to do?

He was going to found a new nation somewhere else.
Found a new nation?
What was he talking about?
He and his wife did not even have any children, and they were getting on in years.
Abraham himself was 75!
What kind of crazy talk was that?

Nevertheless Abraham carried out his decision.

He left Ur of the Chaldees.

He did it because of a spiritual insight—an insight that for him had the authority of a direct command from God.

And God kept His part of the bargain. Abraham was led to Canaan.

In their old age, he and his wife Sarah had a son—Isaac.

> "I will multiply thy seed as the stars of the heaven . . . and in thy seed shall all the nations of the earth be blessed," God had

5

promised.

And it came to pass.

For this pioneer of faith became the father of the Hebrew nation.

And through him, all men everywhere have been blessed—for Jesus Christ Himself was to be one of Abraham's descendants.

Some people find it difficult to believe that human beings like us, like Abraham, can get direct guidance from God,

        can have their lives ordered by Him.

They ask, "But surely you don't believe that God speaks directly,

      specifically,

as I am speaking to you now?

You don't mean that God sends telegrams?"

Now the Bible always speaks of God saying to His children this and that: "And God said unto Abraham . . . "

      "God said unto Moses. . . ."

Was that just for Bible times?

If you have never had an experience of God's guidance in your life, you may question how it comes.

No doubt it comes in various ways to different people.

I cannot fully explain it, but I have to believe it, because I have had many experiences of God's guidance that were for me just as dramatic and critical as the guidance that came to Abraham.

I was given an opportunity to leave Scotland and come to this country, and I asked God what I should do about it.

I asked God in the only way we have to ask Him—through prayer.

I prayed and waited for the answer.

I believed that the answer would come; I did not know when or how.

For three weeks I waited with some impatience, I must confess, and at the end of that time, the answer came, and God told me to go.

I could not accurately describe what was a subjective experience.

I did not see the answer written in the sky, nor yet upon the wall of my room.

But I knew—positively, definitely—that God had said,
"Yes, go."

I remember well the spot where the answer came. It was on a beautiful Sunday afternoon outside Glasgow. I was walking down a path lined with rhododendron on the Sholto-Douglas estate when I heard the voice.
Now, whether it sounded like a voice outside of me or inside of me, I cannot tell.
But I knew it was the voice of God.
I was positive that the answer for which I had prayed had come, and I acted upon it immediately by making application for a visa to enter the United States as a quota immigrant.

Well do I remember on the nineteenth of March, 1927, standing on the afterdeck of the *Cameronia,* watching with moist eyes the purple hills of Mull of Kintyre sinking beneath the screw-threshed waters of the Atlantic, when every turn of the propeller was driving me farther from the land of my birth— from all I knew and loved.

And then—I walked slowly and wonderingly for'ard until I was leaning over the prow.

I stood looking into the west,
    wondering what lay beyond that tumbling
    horizon— wondering what the unknown
    tomorrow held for me.

I, too, was going out in faith, not knowing whither
I went. I was leaving the tube mill, where I had
been working in the machine shop.
I was coming to the United States to enter the min-
istry, because I believed with all my heart that
those were my orders from my Chief.
But I did not know how
        or when
    or where.

I could not foresee the wonderful way in which
God would open doors of opportunity.
I could never have imagined the thrilling way in
which God was to arrange my life . . .

        order my ways
      guide my steps
    provide for all my needs
  give me wonderful friends, generous helpers
until, at last, I would achieve His plan for me, and
be ordained a minister of the Gospel.

It is an amazing adventure simply to be born upon
this wandering island in the sky, to make a tem-
porary home on this rolling ball of matter. . . .
To go to school
    to make friends
      to marry
        to choose a career and to develop it
to rear children and assume life's responsibilities;
to face life with its swift changes of circumstances
that no man can certainly predict an hour ahead—
    These are all adventures.
And it is an adventure to leave it when death calls
and "Taps" sounds for you at the close of life's day.

Each new day is like a hitherto-unvisited country
that we enter—like Abraham leaving Ur for a
strange land—

"Not knowing whither he went."
And every new year we begin a tour of exploration
into twelve months where no man's foot has ever
walked before.
If we all love tales of pioneers, it is because from
the time we are weaned until the time we die—life
is pioneering.
With all his science, with all his new insights and
tools for conquering the unknown, man must face
each day as Paul faced his journey to Rome—"not
knowing the things that shall befall him there."

As you stand peering into the future, you cannot
see what tomorrow will bring.
You cannot even tell as you look upon Grandfather
Time whether his indistinct features are smiling or
frowning. . . .
And his hand behind his back—does it hold

a bouquet
or a brickbat?

Is there no way, then, that we can know the future?
Shall we go—you and I—to some wizened old hag,
cross her palm with silver, and permit her to

spread fanlike before us a deck of cards so that she
may tell us what the future holds?
Shall we listen to her as she interprets a fair lady
or a dark knave as the message of a deuce or a
trey?

Can it be that the drawing of a card will signify the
career we shall follow
        or the person we shall marry
                or the family we shall have?
Nonsense!
There are so many things that even the most edu-
cated among us do not know!
Things that no faculty can teach us . . .
        that no textbooks can contain . . .
                that no man can foresee or prophesy.

I urge you, then, simply to go out in faith—
                                even as Abraham
                                Columbus
                        or the Pilgrim fathers
and all the host of pioneers over the centuries.

Yet this is not easy.
Today we must send young people into a changing
world
        where old concepts are being discarded

old theories exploded
     where standards are constantly
     changing—
into this unknown they must go, whether they like
it or not.

But then is everything so uncertain, you ask?
Is there nothing on which I can rely?

Yes, there is an assurance that can help you to con-
fidently and successfully face the unknown vistas of
all the tomorrows.
It is an assurance given to us in the old Book:

"But I trusted in thee, O Lord: I said, Thou art my
God. My times are in thy hand."   Psalm 31:14-15

If you trust in God, if you are willing to give your
life to Him, then and only then will you have no
fear. For no matter where you go, He will be with
you. You can never wander from the pathway, for
He will lead you.

Some people speak of *luck* and accord it a great
and determining place in their lives.
     They trust to luck,
       they count on it, live by it.

They cross their fingers, knock on wood,
look for four-leaf clovers and carry rabbits' feet.

But I would not dare wish anyone "luck" because
there is no such thing as luck!
Others who speak of "accidents"—and make
allowance for the happening of accidents—regard
certain events as purely accidental.
Yet are there really such things as accidents?

Was the creation of the world an accident?
Are the laws that maintain the universe accidental?
Ask Eddington
        or Jeans
            or Milliken
                or Einstein.

Were the prophecies of the Old Testament acciden-
tal? Was the birth of Jesus Christ an accident?
It was no accident that Judas printed the kiss of
betrayal on the fair cheek of Jesus!
The old rugged cross was no accident!
Paul's conversion was no accident!
The work of Martin Luther was no accident!

Was it an accident that John Wesley was rescued
from a burning house, as his mother described it,
like "the brand plucked from the burning"?

Is this nation of ours an accident?
Were George Washington and the Declaration of
Independence
Abraham Lincoln and the Emancipation Proclama-
tion purely accidental?
Is a rose an accident—merely the coming together
of capricious factors in nature?

I shall not soon forget the words of Dr. W. R. Whitney, a past president of the American Chemical
Society,
      fellow of the American Academy of Arts and
      Sciences,
            director of many vast electrical researches,
            as he made the simplest of all experiments.

Dr. Whitney picked up from his desk a small bar
magnet. He brought this near a steel needle, and
the needle leaped to the magnet.
Why?
Dr. Whitney said:

    "We have worked out elaborate explanations.

We speak learnedly of lines of force. We draw a diagram of the magnetic field.

"Yet we know that there are no lines there and the *field* is just a word to cover our ignorance.
Our explanations are only educated guesses.

"Or consider," Dr. Whitney continued, "the beam of light that comes speeding from a star, traveling hundreds of years. Finally it reaches your optic nerve, and you *see* the star.

"How does that happen?
We have our corpuscular theory of light,
      our wave theory,
            our quantum theory.
But they are all just educated guesses.

"So," explained Dr. Whitney, "after we are all finished with our theories and our guesses, we are still backed up against the fact of God—the will of God at work in what we call 'science.' "
Thus an eminent scientist looked beyond science (that some still think infallible and the source of all answers) for guidance.

Many of our scientific theories and explanations are only educated guesses.
The day before yesterday the atom was thought of as whirling particles, but that is outmoded now.
Yesterday the atom was described as a wave in space, according to Schrödinger's theory; that, too, is outmoded.

Today the atom has been split and developed into one of the greatest explosive forces in the history of mankind.
No, the theory of relativity is not final.
No scientific concept stands still.
All is in motion, because we are forever in the process of discovering more of what God has placed in this world.

But the will of God—the laws we discover
        but cannot always understand

or explain—
the will of God alone is final.
No, there are no accidents.
God is still the ruler of His universe
                    and of our lives,
                    yours and mine.

So, even though you go out, not knowing whither
you go,
            you can go confidently, like Abraham,
provided you can say with the psalmist:

"My times are in Thy hand."

God knows you, and He has a plan for *you*.
God made one you—and only one.
Nobody who ever lived was quite as you are now.
God gave you life for a purpose, and if you fail to
fulfill it, that purpose will never be realized.

I long for all of you to know the full fellowship of
the Christian life . . .
        what it is to be guided by the Lord into the
        very place where He wants you to be . . .
            to know when you make decisions that you
                are doing what He wants you to do.
Not only ministers can find God's will; so too can

                    clerks
                and secretaries
              and engineers
            and waitresses
          and salesmen
and bus drivers.
If you only knew the peace that comes with the
conviction that you are in the place where God
wants you to be . . . and that you are doing the
thing for which He created you.
What a difference it makes!

To Abraham, God spoke directly and specifically.
Nowadays, since the advent of Jesus Christ, I
believe that God speaks to you and me through the
Holy Spirit.
Indeed, we are told in the Scriptures that it is the
function of the Holy Spirit
to guide us
        to lead us into all truth.

So the Holy Spirit is available to guide us in everything:
        A young person into his life's work,
            or into the friendship out of which will
            grow love and marriage to the mate of
            God's choice.

A family can be led to
the city where God
wants them to live.
  A businessperson
  can be guided to make
  the right decisions.
No, that is not silly; it is
not fanaticism.

Nor does it do violence
to human responsibility.
As soon as you try living
this way, you will find
that God's purpose for
your life is maximum
creativity, achievement
and responsibility—not
less.

Others object to the idea that the Lord of the universe could possibly be concerned about the details of millions of lives.
Yet this glorious truth could never have been imagined. Jesus said it was so, and He would never raise false hopes in a human heart.

Jesus' emphasis was always upon the one—the single soul. Consider His parables—

> the story of the lost coin
> of the one lost sheep
> and of the lone lost boy.

"The very hairs of your head are all numbered," He said.

"Your heavenly Father knoweth that ye have need of all these *things*."

In this viewpoint, Jesus was being realistic about human life.
The truth is that our lives are made up of the sum of the small decisions
the little turnings
the minute choices.
If we do not let God into these everyday details, practically speaking we are not letting Him in at all.

Would you like to have God's guidance for your life?

If you would, first you have to believe that He can guide you.

But faith is not belief.

Faith is belief plus what you do with that belief.

I might have believed intellectually that God could guide me, indeed, that I had heard His voice that afternoon in the park. But that would have counted for nothing, had I not gone on to act on that belief by applying for my number as a quota immigrant.

Belief becomes faith only at the point of action.

First of all, if you want to hear God, you will have to face up squarely to the question

"Am I willing to follow His plan wherever it may lead?"

"Am I willing to do whatever He tells me to do?"

This is a decision that must be resolved before you can receive any guidance from God,

before your Christian adventure can begin.

How hard it is for our proud wills to bow the neck
and call Him "Master and Lord"!
Yet bow we must, if we are to understand what life
is all about, if we are to take even the first step
toward maturity

or fulfillment
or greatness.

Understand that this is no craven slavery Christ
asks of us:

"Henceforth I call you not servants; for the
servant knoweth not what his lord doeth; but
I have called you friends."   John 15:15

A friend of Jesus!
No knight of old ever had a greater privilege.
He who bows before this One—joyously to hand
over his life and his future—
finds himself raised to knighthood,
received into the inner circle,
immediately heir to all the rights and
privileges of the King.
But the move is ours. . . .
Are you willing to tell God now that you will follow
His plan wherever it may lead?

This is important because God has given us free
will, and this He will never violate.
He holds in a more profound respect than any of
us could the sanctity of every human personality.
Therefore He requires the consent of our wills
before He will enter our hearts and lives.

And it is just at this point that many of us are in
the grip of a terrible conflict:
We want to hear God speaking to us . . .
  but we are afraid of what we might hear.
We want to be made clean . . .
  but there is still a hunger for the husks the
  swine eat.
We would follow Christ . . .
  but we don't want our friends to think us
  strange.
We want God's way . . .
  but we also want our own way.
There is an answer to our dilemma.
Tell Christ honestly about our divided will . . .
     our divided self.
Ask Him to take that over and make it whole.
And He will!

It may be that His plan for you will not be
revealed for some time.

You will have to keep close to Him, keep listening
for His signals.
His plan for you may be a gradual development.

There are a thousand ways in which He may use
you.
You may have to make some changes in your life,
    break with some of your present companions,
        change some of your habits. . . .
I cannot tell you that—but He can.
He will send His power surging into you,
        to give you power to defeat temptations
      to chase away your fears
    to give you a quiet heart
  to make you joyous and free.

We are living in a hazardous epoch of history.
The wind . . . the earthquake . . . and the fire of
old are here; in fact, the threat of more terrible
fire than man ever thought possible.
It would be a tragedy indeed if the still, small voice
of God's wisdom and direction were not heard at
such a time.
You are leaving port under sealed orders and in a
troubled period.
You cannot know whither you are going or what
you are to do.

But why not take a Pilot on board who knows the nature of your sealed orders from the outset and who will shape your entire voyage accordingly?

He knows the shoals and the sandbanks,
             the rocks and the reefs.
He will steer you safely into that celestial harbor where your anchor will be cast for eternity.
Let His mighty nail-pierced hands hold the wheel, and you will be safe.

Now is a splendid time to entrust your life to Him,
now, as you begin.
Give Him your life.
He will treasure it, even as you.
Then, though you may not know what will be your harbor, you will know your Pilot.
And all will be well.

2

GET OUT OF STEP

One of the memorable scenes in an English novel of some years ago describes how a little boy named Bron goes to church for the first time with his governess.

He watches with interest every part of the service and then the preacher climbs into the high pulpit and Bron hears him give out a piece of terrible news.

It is about a brave and kind Man who was nailed to a cross . . . ferociously hurt a long time ago . . . who feels a dreadful pain even now, because there is something not done that He wants them all to do. Little Bron thinks that the preacher is telling the story because a lot of people are there and they will do something about it.

Bron is sitting impatiently
on the edge of the pew.
He can scarcely wait to see
what the first move will be
in righting this injustice.
But he sits quietly and
decides that after the service someone will do something about it.

Little Bron weeps . . . but
nobody else seems at all
upset.
The service is over, the
people walk away as if they
had not heard such ter-
rible news,
      as if nothing remark-
      able had happened.

As Bron leaves the church,
he is trembling.
His governess looks at him and says:
      "Bron, don't take it to heart—someone will
      think you are strange."

Strange—to be alive and sensitive in one's spirit!
Strange—to show emotion!

30

Strange—to listen to what is going on in God's
house
                                 really to hear
                          to respond!
Strange—to take Jesus Christ seriously!

What does *strange* mean?

The dictionary says, "Differing in some odd way from what is ordinary."
Ought not the Christian, then, be strange?
He should not be satisfied with the ordinary in life.
Christ was not ordinary, and He did not call His followers to be ordinary.

Yet so many people who call themselves Christians today are living ordinary lives.
There is nothing about them that makes them any different from others who make no profession of belief, acknowledge no faith and assume no obligations.
In fact, like Bron's governess, what they fear most in life is being "different."
We are becoming an assembly line society.
The days of rugged individualism that explored the American frontier have been left far behind.

While this pattern of conformity can be seen in every age group, I want to speak about it especially to you young people, because as you huddle together—
    each of you trying to be like everyone else—
you are not finding the satisfactions you seek.

You are still hungry and thirsty on the inside; you
still have problems unsolved, questions un-
answered.
I want to tell you where you can find some of the
answers you seek.

With many of you, conformity has become a creed.
You are terrified at being set apart.
Your own definition of sin is to be out of step with
your friends.

You must wear clothes like everyone else's
      collect and listen to the same music
         learn the same dances
            know the latest slang.

The desire to look and act like everyone else af-
fects all of life:
                  your study habits
              your dating patterns
          how you spend your time
        what you buy with your money
your attitude toward parents . . . your nation . . .
God . . . the church.

In order not to be different, you have to be content
with a low standard of achievement . . .
      a conformity to mediocrity rather than a

desire to excel.

Are you, for example, content with average grades,
because to excel would be to be thought "square"
                        or just plain strange?

Why read for yourself and draw your own con-
clusions when it is far safer to adopt the philosophy
of your friends
                        or favorite columnist
                        or television commentator?
The editorial page of our newspaper is ignored by
too many readers who turn to the sports page or
the comic strips for their reading, because they do
not wish to do any serious thinking.

The teen years are the years for discovering "the
real you,"
        the time when you should be shaping your
        own tastes.
Yet the temptation with all thoughts, activities and
goals is to keep right in step,
        marching along like robots,
                fearful of ridicule . . . criticism . . . isolation
if you should, perchance, get out of step with the
crowd.

Take the matter of social drinking.

More and more this is motivated by the desire to satisfy the requirements of sociability—and too many young people are facing the ultimatum:
"Drink . . . or be left out.

No drink . . .
no dance . . .
no date!"

If you decline a drink, you are accused of assuming a "holier-than-thou" attitude.
You are not a good sport.
You are a wet blanket.
The refusal to drink is often interpreted as a boorish criticism of the occasion and those conducting it.

Social pressure is a dreary fact of our day, and you young people who try to buck it run into embarrassing situations and feel certain tensions that result in strained relationships.

Now it is a natural human desire to be congenial
with the group and to act in harmony with prevail-
ing customs,
and the liquor trade is exploiting it to the limit.

It is this social pressure that induces you to begin
drinking.
It is not because you are thirsty
            or like the taste of alcohol
                    or the smell of it
but simply because you lack the conviction that will
enable you to be "different."
You don't want people to think that you are
"strange."
The drinking required by the powerful pressure of
an authoritative social code is a type of tyranny.
This tyranny of the crowd is actually a flagrant in-
terference with your personal liberty and a gross
repudiation of the democratic principle and spirit.

Why is it that people who want to imbibe alcoholic
beverages insist that you take one, too, just to be so-
ciable?
But do they likewise insist that you are
                    a spoilsport
                a wet blanket
            a prude
if you decline a cup of coffee or prefer a cup of tea?

I am not suggesting that you isolate yourself from
social situations to avoid the embarrassment of
refusing a drink.
Not at all! This was not Jesus' viewpoint.
He Himself was criticized because He associated
with all types and manner of people.
No . . . instead refuse that drink and then show the
others that you can have as much fun as anyone.
In fact, the non-drinker should have more fun, for
alcohol eventually dulls the brain and acts as a
depressant.
I can never understand why the person who acts
on principle should be considered dull.
There is excitement in taking a stand . . . in being
different.
It brings a sparkle to the eyes.
    The mind is alive.
      The spirit sings.
        True values come into sharper focus.

Yet when one falls into line . . . going along with
the crowd, conforming to the group pattern, nothing new is happening!
        There is weary repetition
      dull compliance
    lack of initiative
   boredom.

And that is exactly what so many of you are feeling
and why so many of you are dissatisfied with life.
Have you ever stopped to wonder *why* you have
not wanted to be different?
Is it because you have not found yourself . . .

who you are . . .

why you are here . . .

where you are going?
So you think that your protection and security lies
in huddling together with your friends,

losing your unsure self in the group.
The problem is that by losing yourself in the
group, you can go through your whole life and
never get the answers to what you are supposed to
do with your life.

Then, too, what "everyone else" is doing may be
quite wrong.
Many students cheat, but that does not make cheat-
ing right.
Remember that it is the *mob* that lynches an in-
nocent man.
Entire nations have swallowed evil propaganda
that was all falsehood.
The fact that millions believed it did not turn falsehood into truth or avert disaster.
In fact, what governments decide can be—and
often has been—quite wrong.

Henry Thoreau—a rugged New England individualist of the nineteenth century—once went to jail rather than pay his poll tax to a state that supported slavery.

During this period he wrote his essay "Civil Disobedience"—now famous the world over.

Thoreau's good friend, Ralph Waldo Emerson, hurried to visit him in jail, and peering through the bars exclaimed,

"Why, Henry, what are you doing in there?"

The uncowed Thoreau replied, "Nay, Ralph, the question is, what are you doing out there?"

Who is the strange one: Little Bron—
                          or his governess?
                 Thoreau in jail—
                 or the rest of us outside?

Thoreau was not a churchman because he thought
the churches of his day too convention-bound—
and perhaps he was right.
Yet in his book *Walden* he speaks often of God.
He explains that he went to Walden Pond to live
the simple life because he wanted to get just those
answers that you and I seek:

> "I went to the woods because I wished . . . to
> confront only the essential facts of life and see
> if I could not learn what it had to teach, and
> not, when I came to die, discover that I had
> not lived. . . ."

At another time this amazing man commented:

"If a man does not keep pace with his companions
perhaps it is because he hears a different drummer. Let him step to the music which he hears,
however measured or far away."

Any man or woman who accomplishes anything
worthwhile must have the courage to be different,

even to be regarded as strange, because they are marching to the drumbeat of a Different Drummer and they are not afraid to be out of step.

Abraham Lincoln was one who listened to the Different Drummer, and not to the vindictive voices of his advisers.

Stephens, Phillips and Beecher were among Lincoln's contemporaries who were echoing the cry, "Crush the South. . . .
"Stamp out the whole slave-holding aristocracy. . . .
          Make them pay to the last acre of land
                    the last vestige of power
                              the last drop of blood."

But the great man upon whose furrowed brow the responsibility rested heard a Different Drummer. . .

> "With malice toward none, with charity for all, let us strive on to finish the work we are in, to bind up the nation's wounds . . . to do all which may achieve and cherish a just and lasting peace among ourselves and with all nations."

What is the verdict of today?
Whose words are remembered and repeated—

Lincoln's or Stephens'?

Woodrow Wilson was another.
As a son of the manse, he knew how to listen to the
voice of God, and he was not afraid to take a posi-
tion that other men, hearing no distant drumbeat,
delighted to ridicule.

When Wilson went to Paris after World War I, his
consuming passion was to work out a peace on a
just and righteous basis.
Someone sneered that Wilson talked like Jesus
Christ.
Could there have been a greater compliment paid
to anyone?
But it was not intended as a compliment.

In our day—as in Wilson's—there are many who
are not at all certain that they want to be like
Christ.
Most of their opinions of Him are formed out of
puerile ignorance and a tangle of mistaken concep-
tions.

Yet Christ Himself would be the first to tell you
that this is a central issue you need to face
honestly—
        before you dare call yourself a Christian.

Jesus never deceived anyone about the cost of
following Him.
Over and over He asserted that what He was offer-
ing was hard,
> that a follower had better sit down and count
> the cost before deciding to become one of His
> disciples.
He offers a cross—not a cushion.
He recruits maturity—not spinelessness.

And He would have stern words for the minister
who pleads with people to join his church,
> as if they were doing the church a favor . . .
who sets the requirements for church membership
so low that people can fall over the threshold.

Yet Jesus did not ask us to be different just to make
life hard.
He was thinking of our happiness when He said:

> "Woe unto you, when all men shall speak well
> of you." Luke 6:26

Why, "Woe unto you"?
Isn't it all right to be thought well of?
Isn't popularity a fine thing?

Yes, popularity is pleasant.

I like it as much as you do.
But the truth is no man can have any convictions
          or stand for any principles
        or stick to any standards at all
and be liked by everyone.

Jesus put it this way in John 5:44:

> "How on earth can you believe while you are
> forever looking for each other's approval and
> not for the glory that comes from the one
> God?"

It always amazes me the way people come to
church, participate fully in the prayers and rituals,
nod in agreement during a sermon on faith and
prayer.

Yet if the same people were sitting socially at home
that Sunday evening talking about the problems of
our time—and if someone said impulsively, "Let's
pray about this"—there would be a most uncom-
fortable silence.
The one who suggested prayer would be considered a little strange—different.
We preach about having faith and vision—yet
when somebody shares a daring dream with us
          presents us with an exciting and thrilling

vision
we think he is a bit peculiar.

We hold up certain ideals, and when in society a
young man or a young woman takes a stand for
these ideals, even to the point of making the rest of
us uneasy, we think that he or she is an oddball.

We say that we believe that God can lead people,
and that His guidance is available in everything. . .
.
Yet when certain people try to seek His guidance
in planning a vacation
     in picking a college
        or in selecting friends
we conclude that they are strange.
There is another reason why Jesus said,

    "Woe unto you when all men speak well of
    you."

As our fear about others' approval grows,
our freedom shrinks.
We can see this at its most extreme in the
totalitarian state.
The totalitarian state cannot exist unless it is com-
posed of deindividualized persons.

There the citizen gives up one of Christianity's most outstanding characteristics: the freedom of choice.

It is literally true that only in God's will do we have the chance to find ourselves, to be persons. Therefore only in God's will do we have real freedom.
Today the world has a desperate need of people who are willing to be different.

In Bernard Shaw's play *St. Joan,* some soldiers are talking about the "Maid of Orleans."
One of them says, "There is something about the girl. . . . Her words and her ardent faith in God have put fire into me."
His captain replies, "Why, you are almost as mad as she is."
And the soldier stubbornly goes on, "Maybe that's what we need nowadays—mad people.
See where the sane ones have landed us."

If it is sanity that has brought the world to its present state . . .
> if it is sanity that has produced the social order in which we live . . .

then I for one am willing to give madmen a chance.
I believe we need people who are different.

All those who have carried civilization forward
have been angry men—grousing in the public
parks and the marketplaces, nailing denunciations
up on public buildings.
They knew they were in a conflict, and they took
the wrongs in society—yes, and the wrongs in the
church—
        terribly to heart.

We need such people who will carry their faith
into the office
                into Congress
            into society
            into the school
        into the home . . .
people who will be different even if it will cost
them their social popularity
        their economic fortunes
            or their very lives.

But one does not get that kind of faith except by a
personal friendship with Jesus Christ.
Then He will tell you what to do.
        You will be sure of your ground.
            With His hand on your shoulder, you will
            have no fear of the opinions of other
            people.

Easy? Of course it is not easy.
I think too much of the youth today to offer you a
sugar-coated Christianity.
That would betray my Lord.

It would also not be worthy of your great potential.
Deep in your hearts you look with longing toward
the heights.
You know that there will be rugged terrain
                    panting lungs
                aching legs
but also the cool, clean upper air and the exhilara-
tion of gaining the summit at last
        of achieving vision and perspective.

God's marching orders always involve sacrifice and courage.
The drumbeat of the Different Drummer calls for bravery.
It is not for dancing.
It does not appeal to the blood—but to the heart of a person.
It calls for will and sacrifice.
It is a stirring drum, and they who hear it are always in a minority.
Those who answer it may perchance hear the words of a new Beatitude. . . .

"Blessed are they who are thought strange,
for they have taken the Gospel to heart."

3

DAWN CAME TOO LATE

Have you ever come right up to the point of making a decision and then backed away—
to your regret later on?
Perhaps it was the chance to land a new job
to go on a trip
to propose marriage
to take a strong stand.

The moment confronted you, made your heart beat faster. You paused . . . but did not act . . . and then it was too late.

Circumstances changed.
The opportunity never came again in quite the same way.
I have seen this happen when a person comes under Jesus' spell.

Suddenly he sees his life through Christ's eyes.
He knows that his life is off center, purposeless.
He feels trapped in wrongdoing.
He lacks zest.
He has clutched at happiness but it has eluded him.
Then he is offered the adventure of commitment to Christ.
Something stirs in him, like a bugle call to action.
He clears his throat, almost speaks, starts to move.
Then a counterforce steps in: "Don't be hasty," it says.
"Let's not do anything foolish."
"Watch out for embarrassment."
"There's plenty of time to think it over."
But that particular moment slips by and is gone forever.
He was on the brink of a move that would have changed everything.
He was nearly Christ's—so close to greatness.

But nearly is not enough.

It has happened so from the dawn of time.
The story of Nicodemus is the story of such a man.

He might have been a disciple—but was not.

Nicodemus was a member of the Sanhedrin—the
highest Jewish court.
The label John gave Nicodemus has stuck:
> "Nicodemus, which at the first came to Jesus
> by night."
Why did Nicodemus wait until it was dark?
Was he, perchance, afraid?

Suppose Nicodemus came while it was night
simply because he could wait no longer.
Suppose he had come—without wasting a minute—
> immediately after he had seen Christ for the
> first time?

Nicodemus knew the spot well.
He had sometimes sought refreshment of the spirit
there himself when he could no longer stand
either the heat of Jerusalem
> or its seething intrigue.

The tall man drew his beautiful outer cloak of
striped linen more closely about his shoulders.
It was frosty at night on the Judean hills.
He paused on the brow of Olivet to look out across
the moonlit valley.
The Temple, which Herod was still rebuilding for
the Jews, towered over the valleys of Jehoshaphat
and Hinnom,

gleaming like snow
in the moonlight.
Nicodemus sighed in-
voluntarily as he looked
down at the city.
Asleep, Jerusalem
looked peaceful enough.

But awake? It was a
dirty city . . .
a desperate city. . . .
The dignified aristocrat
knew only too well the
machinations at its
heart.
The Nazarene—
whether He knew it or
not—was in real danger
of His life.

Stepping out of the
shadows, Nicodemus
found Christ exactly
where Joseph had said he would.
Strangely, the Master seemed not at all surprised
to see him. In fact, it was almost as if He were
expecting Nicodemus.

They talked for hours—those two—totally un-
aware of the passing of time.
There was a meeting of minds such as Nicodemus
had never known, even in his youth, with his
greatest teachers from Jerusalem, Corinth, or
Alexandria.

In the Lord of Life, this master of Israel discovered
fathomless depths of mind and heart.
Nicodemus knew men.
Here is no cheap fanatic, he thought.
Here are clear eyes and a quiet voice.
  Here is Manhood at its highest.

The talk was of spiritual regeneration—being born
again, but this time, not a natural but a super-
natural birth.
A change in the inner man, without which no man
can get into the Kingdom of God.

At this point, Nicodemus asked what any one of us
might have asked,

  "How can a man be born when he is old?"
           John 3:4

You and I have voiced the same doubts in different
ways.
Suppose Jesus asks us to give up something we
want to keep—
We want to have our fun first.
"Besides, there's plenty of time."
But is there?
How do we know that there is plenty of time?

56

Or we have answered in another way.
"I am what I am—nobody special.
Even though I'm still young, I have deeply
ingrained habits,

       not all of them good.
It just doesn't seem reasonable that I should begin
all over again and be somebody else.
Besides, who wants to be good?
I'm just not built that way."

And Jesus answered, "Of course you're not built
that way. I'm not talking about a little repair work
here and there

     a little increase in kindness
    a bit more generosity.
Something much more drastic is required."

"Ye must be born again"—not by education
   or culture
    or legislation
    but by regeneration.

But Nicodemus' was the voice of man's skeptical
questioning: "How can a man be born again?"

And Jesus answered quietly. Yes, there is a mystery
here, Nicodemus, that you are not quite ready to
understand.

"The wind bloweth where it listeth, and thou hearest the sound thereof, but canst not tell whence it cometh, and whither it goeth: so is every one that is born of the Spirit."

John 3:8

There are many things going on around us which we do not understand and cannot explain
but they are nonetheless true and valid.

There are some things in the Christian life about which it is useless to argue, for they can never be proved by logic.
I do not fully understand regeneration.
But I have seen it take place.

I have seen men and women changed from above — completely.
Men reclaimed from habitual drunkenness to sobriety. . . .
Criminals changed into respectable citizens. . . .

58

I have seen egocentrics become outgoing, from
grasping, greedy materialists into the spiritually
minded, suddenly aware of the winds of the Spirit.
And then Nicodemus asked, "How can these things
be?"
Perhaps he meant, "Oh, yes, I see.

                    All right, I believe You.
I believe that it is possible for a man to start all
over.
But how? Tell me how?
How does a man begin? What does one do first?"

And then Jesus answered and said unto him—
probably with a twinkle in His eyes—
"Art thou a master of Israel, and knowest not these
things?"
You, a leader of the people and don't know?
You, a teacher and interpreter of the Sacred Law
and you don't know how?
"It isn't something we can do for ourselves,
Nicodemus.
Only God can work this miracle.

      He has to do it for us.
All that is required of us is our willingness to have
Him make us over.
He requires only our permission.
Our Father never violates a person's freedom of
choice.

He wants for His heirs only those who long to be.

"You see, Nicodemus, it is the old self-centered ego
in us . . .
                              vain
                    critical of other people
                         wanting its own way . . .
                              that is what has to go.
"It's painful character-surgery, painful—
but necessary.
We can give God permission to slay that self-
centered person in us, and He will.
Then the Spirit of God will come to live in us
                         giving us a new nature
                    a new set of desires
               a new way of looking at things
          even a new will.
                              That is being born again."

Perhaps there was sadness in Christ's eyes as He
made the strange statement that somehow, in
order to achieve this rebirth, He—this Jesus—
must be lifted up from the earth.

It was beyond Nicodemus, too mysterious, this talk
of the blowing wind,
          blowing from the Unknown
          into the Undiscoverable. . . .

These beautiful words, like the music of the
spheres,
falling upon his ears:

> "For God so loved the world, that he gave his
> only begotten Son, that whosoever believeth in
> him should not perish, but have everlasting
> life. "   John 3:16

Christ must have felt an affinity
        a great affection for this man Nicodemus.
For it was your visit, Nicodemus, which gave us
that precious revelation; your talk drew it forth.

You came out of your night—and a shaft of light
pierced it.
You came out of your night, and now the dawn is
breaking.

The two men fell silent, bound together by
thoughts lying beyond the ability of words.
They stood . . . looking down across twenty miles
of hilltops, watching the sun come up behind the
blue hills of Moab, the misty hills.
And in the distance, cocks began to crow.

"I must be going," said Nicodemus suddenly.
He looked into Christ's eyes and gripped His hand.

With long strides, the tall man retraced his steps
down the rocky, winding path with the parting
words of Jesus still ringing in his ears—words like
an echo out of eternity:

> "Light has entered the world, Nicodemus, but
> anyone whose life is evil will avoid it; but one
> whose life is true will come to it, fearing it
> not. . . . Men have preferred darkness to light.
> It is their choice; You and I know, Nicodemus,
> that their decision is already made."

So the Master knew.
He knew. . . .

Time passed.
It was now late in September—the time of the
Feast of Tabernacles.
Many things had happened since that night when
Nicodemus had first come to the Galilean.
Many people had been healed
　　many miracles wrought
　　　　many words spoken
　　　　　　many prayers uttered.
many plots hatched, many schemes perfected.

The Pharisees were increasingly troubled by the following Jesus had attracted because of His miracles.
Many of the common folk were actually beginning to believe that He was, indeed, the Messiah—even as He had said.
That would not do!

On the last day of the Feast, the 71 members of the Sanhedrin solemnly assembled in the great Hall of Hewn Stone in the Temple.
Caiaphas had called them into session.
The question was: "What shall we do with Jesus?"

The discussion rose and fell like waves around the semicircle of distinguished men.
Caiaphas seemed impatient of discussion.
It was apparent that he wanted Christ put to death.
But some said, "Not yet. On what basis could you condemn Him now?"
Others sided with Caiaphas.

Anger—a quiet, cold anger—welled up in Nicodemus.
He was hearing once again the faint sigh of wind through cypress trees
　　　feeling a hand on his shoulder
　　　　　seeing the pink dawn beyond a distant

hillside,
hearing a quiet voice saying, "But he that doeth
truth cometh to the light."

Suddenly Nicodemus felt that his own future was
not important.
Did it matter what his compatriots thought of him?
Nothing mattered except honesty
                    fairness
                justice
            truth.
And Nicodemus rose from his stone chair and
pulled himself to his full height.
A voice, calm, clear, used to controlling other men,
rang out through the marble hall:

"Surely our Law does not condemn the
accused before listening to his defense, calling
reputable witnesses, and ascertaining the full
truth."

Caiaphas rose in his place—mockery in his eyes,
a sneer on his lips:

"Are you a Galilean too? Nothing good comes
out of Galilee. I'm surprised at you, sir. Is this
some kind of September madness of yours?"

Nicodemus did not reveal to the Sanhedrin that he
was willing to stand with Christ whatever
happened.
He did not announce that he was willing to follow
Him and trust Him all the rest of the way.
No—he did not do that. But he had spoken!
He had sought to defend Him on a point of Jewish
law! He had taken one step toward the light!

There was a strange peace in the heart of
Nicodemus.
Already he felt those eyes, warm and appreciative,
smiling upon him.

Only once more do we see Nicodemus.

It is near the end of the narrative, some five
months later.
The scheming Caiaphas has had his way: Judas
had played into his hands.

The Master had mounted His last pulpit . . .
        preached His last sermon.
The beggars waiting by the gates of Jerusalem
would still need their crutches and sticks, for He
who might have freed them from dependence on
those extra legs was Himself dead.

After hatred had finished its work, "Joseph of
Arimathaea, being a disciple of Jesus, but secretly
for fear of the Jews, besought Pilate that he might
take away the body of Jesus: and Pilate gave him
leave" (John 19:38).

He had prepared a rock-hewn tomb that the
Master might be interred with love and tenderness
and that deep inarticulate sorrow which had
stunned the little band of believers.

Joseph "came therefore, and took the body of
Jesus. And there came also Nicodemus, which at
the first came to Jesus by night, and brought a mix-
ture of myrrh and aloes, about an hundred pound
weight. Then took they the body of Jesus, and

wound it in linen clothes with the spices" (John 19:38-40).

"And there came also Nicodemus. . . ."
There is a sob in John's words.

Nicodemus, who first came by night, now comes in daylight.
But it is too late.
He can do nothing for the Master now except lavish the spices on His body, and wish that he might have saved Him.

The Master had said that it was hard for a rich man to get into the Kingdom.
  So Nicodemus had found it. . . .
    He had much to lose by taking a definite stand.
But he should have had the courage;
    now he knew it.

There in the Sanhedrin he should have said, "Yes, I am one of His disciples. I believe that what He says is true. I had a long talk with Him. I have never met a saner Man
      a kinder Man
     a wiser Man.
   Go ahead, excommunicate me, too.

I intend to stand with the Galilean to the end."

Instead he had taken but one timid step toward the light, and that had not been enough to stem the dark tide.

Nicodemus might have stood with John, there at the foot of the cross, when the others crouched at the fringe of the crowd, ready to run at the first sign of danger.

When the others forsook Him and fled, Nicodemus might have been there . . . stood by Him, for the sake of that night when they had together watched the dawn come up over the hills of Moab.

Now it was too late.
>The Master was dead.
>>"And there came also Nicodemus. . . ."
>>His tears lay on the white linen like diamonds.

Many of you—like Nicodemus—have come close to Jesus.
Perhaps you too have felt the nudge
>the uneasy feeling in your own conscience
>>the tugging at the heart

the resolves that spring up
the longing to do something special
to *be* someone.
Could not that be Christ calling you?

And you have waited. . . .
You wanted to respond
but you waited.

Remember that He will not force Himself upon
you. He will not assault you, or intrude where He
is not wanted.

Christ will let you go through the years, using no
restraint or compulsion beyond the appeal that He
is making constantly —
to your better nature
your loyalty
your gratitude
your recognition of the imperish-
ables
the hunger of your own heart.

There are some terrible scenes in the Gospel
narrations:
Jesus standing and letting the rich young ruler
walk away from Him.

And if the Gadarenes prefer their swine to His
company, He does not argue the point.
He enters the boat again. . . .
    The wind fills the sails.
        Slowly the vessel draws out.
            He goes as silently as He came.

If the inhospitable Samaritans do not want Him,
He punishes them in a far more terrible way than
the disciples suggested:
They were for calling down fire from heaven on
them.

Jesus does something more awful. . . .
He simply passes on and leaves them.

An hour may come when you will never again
hear Christ's knock on your heart's door.
Everything that happens to you from now on—in
this life and throughout eternity—hinges on
whether or not you stretch out your hand to open
the door to Him.
The latch is on the inside.

Just one more step, Nicodemus.
Just one more step to take.
The dawn is coming.
It must not come . . . too late!

4

THE RISK OF REACH

It was an afternoon in the early summer; there was a strange quiet on the battlefield.

In the bright sunshine, the air was balmy and had a breath of garden in it.

By some grotesque miracle, a bird was singing somewhere near at hand.

On the firing step, with his rifle lying in a groove in the parapet, stood a private soldier in field-gray, his uniform stained with mud and blood.

On his face, so young yet strangely marked with the lines of war that made him look old, was a wistful faraway expression.

He was enjoying the sunshine and the quiet of this strange lull in the firing.

The heavy guns had been silent—there was no sound to break the eerie stillness.

Suddenly a butterfly fluttered into view and alighted on the ground al-most at the end of his rifle.

It was a strange visitor to a battleground—

so out of place—
so out of keeping with
the grim setting
rifles and bayonets
barbed wire and parapets
shell holes and twisted bodies.

But there it was—a gorgeous creature, the wings
like gold leaf splashed with carmine,
swaying in the warm breath of spring.

As the war-weary youngster watched the butterfly,
he was no longer a private in field-gray.
He was a boy once more, fresh and clean, swinging
through a field in sunny Saxony, knee-deep in
clover
                    buttercups
                and daisies.

That strange visitor to the front-line trench
recalled to him the joys of his boyhood, when he
had collected butterflies.
It spoke to him of days of peace.
It was a symbol of the lovelier things of life.
It was the emblem of the eternal, a reminder that
there was still beauty and peace in the world—that
somewhere there was color and fragility
                and perfume
            and flowers
        and gardens.

He forgot the enemy a few hundred yards across
no man's land.
He forgot the danger and privation and suffering.
He forgot everything as he watched that butterfly.

With all the hunger in his heart,
with the resurrection of dreams and visions that he
thought were gone, he reached out his hand
toward that butterfly.

His fingers moved slowly, cautiously, lest he
frighten away this visitor to the battlefield.
In showing one kind of caution, he forgot another.
The butterfly was just beyond his reach—so he
stretched, forgetting that watchful eyes were waiting for a target.

He brought himself out slowly—with infinite care
and patience—until now he had just a little distance to go. He could almost touch the wings that
were so lovely.

And then—ping . . . *ing* . . . *ing* . . . *ing*. . . .
A sniper's bullet found its mark.
The stretching fingers relaxed . . .
        the hand dropped flat on the ground.
For the private soldier in field-gray, the war was
over.

An official bulletin issued that afternoon said that
        "All was quiet on the Western Front."
And for the boy in field-gray it was a quiet that no
guns would ever break.

There is always a risk—when you reach for the
beautiful.
When you reach out for the lovelier
                    finer
                    more fragrant things of life—
there is always a risk—and you can't escape it.

The risk is what makes the Christian life exciting.
        It is thrilling—make no mistake about it.
            It is an adventure.
As long as we live in this world, there will always
be a risk in reach.

But there are many in our time who are
abnormally afraid of that risk of reach.
They are afflicted with a modern disease.
The psychiatrists have ponderous names for the
sundry phobias that afflict us poor humans . . .
and the names are as terrible as the disease.

Agoraphobia is the fear of open spaces,
while claustrophobia is the fear of being shut in,
and acrophobia is the fear of heights.
There are many people who are afraid to climb
and they will not leave the ground . . .
        to get out on the roof of a building
            or up in a tower
                or on a mountain.

To be up on any elevation and look down makes
them dizzy
    affects their sense of balance
    strikes terror into their hearts.
They are afraid of that which is high.
They have acrophobia.

But acrophobia is not only the fear of
                high monuments
             mountains
        and flights in airplanes.
    It may also be the fear of high ideals
      high thoughts
        high ambitions.

There are timid souls who avoid high places
because they are afraid. . . .
But then there are others who avoid high ideals
because they are content with low ones.
There are persons who do not have high ambitions
because they are lazy.
Altogether there are a great many people afflicted
with acrophobia.
Are you?

Not enough of you today are hitching your wagons
to stars.
You think it enough to couple a trailer to your car.

Jesus remarked upon those who sought the small
and shallow things of life,

"Verily I say unto you, They have their reward."
Matthew 6:2

That is, they got what they went after, and that is
all they will ever get.
That is what they deserve.
They take a tin thimble to the ocean and scoop up
a few drops, for that is all they can get into a
thimble.
It isn't the fault of the ocean they did not get more,
that they did not plunge in and swim in the ocean's
immensity.

The tragedy of this age is that people with minds
to think and souls that are hungry are so afraid to
reach up and seek the things that are high.
What a tragedy that personalities in the glorious
twentieth century are afflicted with acrophobia.

The night sky does something to the stargazer.
One does not remain the same after seeing a sunset
or gazing into the heart of a flower
or watching the tiny fledglings in a nest.

There is a silent uplifting importation from the

Absolute.
It does us good to look up and see Orion driving
his hunting dogs across the Zenith. . . .
Or Andromeda shaking out her tresses over limit-
less space.

It enlarges the self to have studied great architec-
ture
to know great art—the reds of Titian
        the sunsets of Turner
       the seas of Winslow Homer—
to have trembled with the passion of Romeo
or the tenderness of Francis of Assisi
to have wrestled with Kant's categorical impera-
tives,
the whirring of angels' wings in Milton's *Paradise
Lost,* to have been swept away on the surge of
music in Beethoven
to have engraved upon the heart the prologue to
John's Gospel
to march with the majestic affirmations of the
Nicean Creed.

It does something inside a man.
It stretches him mentally
    stirs him morally
      inspires him spiritually.
He is a bigger man—sweeter, nobler, higher

richer than he was before.

The uplift of adoration brings the humble but blessed beholder to the threshold of a worship which miraculously transforms him just by beholding.

Out of the horrors of World War II came an expression of such worship—a poem written by a nineteen-year-old flyer who met his death serving with the Royal Canadian Air Force. His father was an Episcopal rector whom I knew in Washington. Pilot-Officer John Gillespie Magee, Jr., called his poem "High Flight."

"Oh, I have slipped the surly bonds of earth,
And danced the skies on laughter-silvered wings.
Sunward I've climbed, and joined the tumbling mirth
Of sun-split clouds—and done a hundred things
You have not dreamed of—wheeled and soared and swung
High on the sunlit silence. Hov'ring there,
I've chased the shouting wind along, and flung
My eager craft through footless halls of air.

"Up, up the long, delirious, burning blue,
I've topped the windswept heights with easy grace

Where never lark, or even eagle flew—
And, while with silent, lifting mind I've trod
The high untrespassed sanctity of space,
Put out my hand and touched the face of God."

The Christian is to seek the things above—to seek
them
> as the needle seeks the pole . . .
> as the sunflower seeks the sun . . .
> as the river seeks the sea . . .
> as the eagle seeks the ceiling of the world.

That was why Paul pleaded with the first-century
Christians to set their affections on things above . . .
> high things
> lofty concepts
and "not on the things of the earth."

But it is so difficult for us to transfer our affections,
for we have fallen in love with toyland
> and our playthings have become so dear.

It is so difficult for us to believe the truth: that this
life is but a preparation for a greater and more
glorious one to come . . . and that if we would only
believe,
> if we only had enough faith and the right kind
> and were seeking the "things above,"

then all our real needs—earth's trinkets for which we strive so desperately—would be provided for us.

Once and for all, we must put out of our minds that the purpose of life here is to enjoy ourselves
      to have a good time
   to be happy
 to make money
and to live in ease and comfort.

That is not what life is all about.
You were put here for a purpose, and that purpose is not related to superficial pleasures.
No one owes you a living—not your parents, not your government, not life itself.
You do not have a right to happiness.
You have a right to nothing.
I believe that God wants us to be happy—but it is not a matter of *our right,* but of *His love and mercy.*

The time for drifting
        or sleeping
      or wishful thinking
or daydreaming is over.
The state of our world today makes that a very
dangerous pastime.

This generation of young people and all of you
who are sensitive to what is going on around you,
are called to a supreme adventure.
There is a great stirring in society.
The upheavals of life and the revolutions of multi-
tudes across the world in desperate motion are
indications that our world can never be the same
again.

So do not ever underestimate what you can do.
You have the courage to cast off your acrophobia
        and to dream big
      and to aim high—
if you do it with God's help.

Two years before I left Scotland, I had a small part
in a remarkable demonstration of what youthful
vision combined with Christian faith can
accomplish.

Bert Patterson was a medical student in Glasgow
University, very much in love with Nessie Knight.
They had been friends through high school.
They were wholesome young people, interested in
life and eager to invest their personalities to some
noble end.
Both belonged to a group of about twenty of us
who went around together.
We played football and cricket.
The girls had a hockey team.
We went to picnics together . . . took hikes. . . .
Normal young people—fond of life
                    full of fun
with some of the virtues and most of the faults of
young people anywhere.

At last Bert was graduated. . . .
          secured his medical degree and volunteered
          to go to Africa as a medical missionary.
Before he left, he and Nessie were married.
Leaving his wife at home, he then went out to
establish the Scotch Presbyterian Medical Mission
at Sulenkama, Africa.

Bert knew there was nothing in Africa for him but
a grass hut and a tremendous need.
He determined to build a hospital
                    a dispensary

and a compound
before he could ask Nessie to come out to help him
in his work.

To those of us who were left behind there came the
challenge to do what we could to build that hospital and dispensary for them in Africa.

Bert had gone out like a happy warrior to tramp
the high road of service and sacrifice. . . .
Surely there was something we at home could do.

Money was scarce. . . .

Mission committees were hard up. . . .
    The churches were giving all they could
    but there were so many needs.

Now Nessie was quite small, but her heart was big,
and she had the spirit of a giant.
She organized us into a dramatic club to raise the
money needed to build the hospital.
She was director and coach
        organizer and leader
of one of the craziest, maddest and most thrilling
ventures with which I have ever been connected.

We decided to present two plays by Sir James
Barrie—*Quality Street* and *Dear Brutus*.
We determined to present the plays in one of
Glasgow's downtown theaters—the Coliseum—and
to hire it for a week.

It was a fantastic sort of thing, I must admit, to
think that a gang of twenty young people could
hire a theater for a week, and do a good job of
presenting such challenging plays . . .
        to do it in such a way as to raise enough
        money to built a hospital in Africa.
Nevertheless, I can only tell you what happened.

Sir James Barrie presented to us an autographed
copy of the plays that they might be auctioned and
the money applied to the fund.
Sir Horace Fellowes, a noted conductor, not only
agreed to let his orchestra play, but he himself
came on the opening night to conduct.

Each one of us sold tickets frantically for weeks
before the production.
We enlisted all our friends in schools and in offices
       in restaurants and in movie theaters
     in the university and in churches
   in the stores and in the tramcars.
We secured the help of the newspapers.
There was something about the whole mad
enterprise that captivated our fathers and mothers.

Suffice it to say that the plays were successful
beyond our dreams.
The young people acted as if they were inspired,
and who can say they weren't?
And every night for a week hordes of people came
to the Coliseum theater and caught the spirit of it
all, so that in the end enough money was sent out
to Bert to build his dispensary and a compound—a
place for him to work and live.
And Nessie went out to Africa at the close of the
year to join him in God's work.

Nor does the story end there.
The next year Nessie's sister, Jean, directed
another of Barrie's plays, *Mary Rose,* and played
the lead herself to raise enough money this time to
build a hospital.

One of the Glasgow newspapers in telling the story
called Bert and Nessie "Pilgrims of the Lonely
Way."
But I wonder if their way is so lonely after all!

Pilgrims of the Lonely Way . . . Pilgrims unafraid
to reach. . . .
They are in good company.
There are great people who walk beside them—a
rich fellowship dedicated to hard labor and austere
lives in far-off places.
But the excitement
    the joy
      the adventure
        the deep inner satisfactions
of those who dare to reach sky-high more than
make up for any loneliness.

For no way can be lonely if it is the way Christ
walks.
No way can be lonely if it is the way to which He
calls you.